An American Family Foundation Book

EXIT COUNSELING

A Family Intervention

About the Author

Carol Giambalvo has worked as an exit counselor since 1983, after five years' membership in est and The Hunger Project. She served on the national Board of Directors of the Cult Awareness Network from 1988 to 1991 and as National Coordinator of FOCUS (a national support network for former cult members) for four years. She presently serves on the FOCUS Board of Directors and is Chairperson of the American Family Foundation's Ex-member Outreach Study Group. She has appeared on many national and local TV and radio programs to discuss and debate the cult issue in our society. She has written numerous articles, including her personal story. She lives with her husband, Noel, in Florida.

Praise for *Exit Counseling: A Family Intervention*

"When families seek help in dealing with a loved one in a cult, they usually have no idea about their options or where to turn. An experienced, ethical, and very successful exit counselor, Giambalvo explains all the steps involved, her philosophy, and the goal of the process: informed choice. She makes clear how an ethical family intervention done in collaboration with an experienced exit counselor evolves. This book will allow families to read and learn about the educational interchanges in which they and their cultist loved one will participate. A book of this quality has long been needed—not just for families but also for mental health professionals, clergy, and the public."
—Margaret T. Singer, Ph.D., Emeritus Adjunct Professor,
Dept. of Psychology, University of California, Berkeley

"The clearest and most down-to-earth advice on exit counseling available, this book demystifies a process that is often shrouded in mystery."
—Arnold Markowitz, M.S.W., Director, Cult Clinic and Hotline,
Jewish Board of Family and Children's Services, New York City

"Aside from the issue of mind control itself, the most mystifying concept to families of cultists is that of an exit counseling. Families considering an intervention to help a cult member are unsure what happens during an exit counseling, how it works, and what their role is to be. In this excellent book, Giambalvo demystifies the phenomenon and explains in a step-by-step manner just what to expect before, during, and after an exit counseling. This book contains information that is not available in written form anywhere else. It fills an information gap that has existed for years. We highly recommend it."
—Lorna Goldberg, A.C.S.W., and William Goldberg, A.C.S.W.

"Carol Giambalvo is a very competent counselor with unique skills for helping cult-affected families. Her book is a succinct description of the procedures that she has used effectively in numerous interventions. *Exit Counseling: A Family Intervention* will be a source of information and hope for many as they seek deliverance from the shackles of mind control."
—David J. Mahan, Ed.D., public school superintendent,
and parent of a former cultist

"This book offers a sensitive and balanced approach to dealing with a family member who has been "captured" by a cult. What's more, it works. Giambalvo's strategy of involving and counseling the entire family, combined with the nonthreatening presentation of alternative information to the cultist, creates an atmosphere of support and mutual respect, enhancing the potential for a successful intervention and minimizing the emotional wrenching that characterizes many of the aggressive "deprogramming" techniques.

The author is an expert in her field, a veteran of countless interventions, and her experiences have prepared her well for knowing what to expect from a cultist and for developing effective and humanistic responses. Our family is enormously grateful for Carol's help, and that of her husband Noel, in dealing with our cult experience. We hope that her book will be of comfort and assistance to others who find themselves in similar circumstances."

—Stephen C. Reiner, businessman, attorney,
and father of a former cultist

"Giambalvo superbly defines the process of exit counseling, while providing invaluable practical information and advice for those considering such an intervention. Her work is a 'must read' for the layman and professional alike who is interested in helping a cultist re-evaluate his or her situation."

—M. Keith Mader, M.S.W., psychotherapist and former cultist

"*Exit Counseling* answers virtually every question a concerned parent or loved one may have concerning how to proceed with an exit counseling. Giambalvo effectively takes the mystery and fear out of a normally confusing, often traumatic, situation by providing a clear, concise, logical framework for further action."

—Todd Hohman, former member of the Boston Church of Christ

"Carol Giambalvo is one of the leading authorities in the field of exit counseling, who speaks not only from experience as an exit counselor but also as an ex-member of a cult. The approach she presents here provides a rational, well researched guide to a confusing and often frightful situation. Giambalvo outlines a method that allows for the integrity and respect of the cultist as well as all the other participants. I would highly recommend that anyone facing the involvement of a love one in a cult read this book!"

—Nancy Miquelon, National Coordinator, FOCUS (Former Cult Members' Support network)

"This book is the most helpful step-by-step process of exit counseling available. Anyone planning to help his or her child or loved one leave a cult must read this book. One need not look anywhere else for an explanation of the exit counseling process—it's all here in one volume."

—Paul Martin, Ph.D., Director of Wellspring Retreat & Resource Center

EXIT COUNSELING

A Family Intervention

Carol Giambalvo

American Family Foundation

For information, write
American Family Foundation
P.O. Box 2265
Bonita Springs, FL 33959.

This book is a revised, second edition of *Exit Counseling: A Family Intervention*, copyright © 1991, Carol Giambalvo.

Since each case and each individual are different, the material contained herein is not offered as a uniform method for conducting a family intervention, nor is it always successful. In evaluating the alternatives available to them and appropriate courses of conduct, families and concerned individuals are advised to consult helping professionals, clergy, and legal counsel.

Library of Congress Catalog Card No: 92-081593

ISBN 0-931337-03-8

Printed in the United States of America

10 9 8 7 6 5 4 3 2 1

ACKNOWLEDGMENTS

I wish to express my gratitude to the many people who helped in the writing of this book: William Goldberg, M.S.W., A.C.S.W., and Lorna Goldberg, M.S.W., A.C.S.W., edited the first version; Sandy Andron, Ed.D., offered many suggestions and helped edit the first version; Noel Giambalvo for his constant support, love, and patience; Michael Langone, Ph.D., for his support and for editing this revised edition; and Janja Lalich for her skills in manuscript preparation.

My heartfelt appreciation goes to Lorna and Bill Goldberg, who selflessly for over seventeen years have opened their home and their hearts to offer their professional skills in giving support and loving guidance to countless former members in the New York/New Jersey FOCUS support group. Personal gratitude goes to them for their help in my own recovery process.

Much thankfulness and affection go to those colleagues in exit counseling with whom I have worked and who have shared their knowledge, skills, and expertise in this budding field. They have all contributed in their own way to this book.

And sincere gratitude to all the families and clients I have worked with over the years. Their insights and feedback have helped me develop abilities to help others better. I don't know of another field where an individual has the opportunity to meet such wonderful, courageous people who demonstrate their love in the most stressful of situations. Time and again such families have shown their willingness to go the extra mile; they have renewed my faith in the strength of the unconditional love that bonds families.

An acknowledgment page without mentioning the American Family Foundation and the Cult Awareness Network would be empty indeed. To the boards, administrators, professionals, supporters, and families who are part of these organizations I offer my deepest thanks. Seldom does one find a group of individuals from all walks of life, all faiths, all points of view who work together unceasingly and lovingly. Repeatedly families tell me of the support and care they received from these "perfect strangers." Families don't have to tell me—I've experienced it firsthand. I owe my recovery to them. I've gleaned wisdom from them. I draw the strength, knowledge, and courage to do this work from them. Thank you!

CONTENTS

PREFACE

This book was written to dispel the myths and the aura of magical solution surrounding the process of family interventions related to exit counseling.

Family intervention specialists knowledgeable about cults and mind control have inherited the label "exit counselors" from the network of individuals and organizations providing information on cults. The term *exit counselor* originally came into favor in order to distinguish voluntary interventions with cultists from "deprogramming," which was associated with physical restraint of cultists (e.g., refusing to let the cultist leave the family's home until he or she had listened to a deprogrammer). "Exit counseling," however, does not adequately describe most voluntary interventions today. "Counseling" often connotes a systematic attempt to help clients change their behavior. Most exit "counselors," on the other hand, focus on sharing information rather than changing behavior, although clients may change their behavior as a result of the information they receive.

I believe that the terms *cult information specialist* or *cult information consultant* better describe what most exit counselors do. But since the term *exit counseling* is so widespread, I use it in the body of this book, even though I would prefer to use other terminology. For now, I believe that popular usage compels us to use the term *exit counseling*, despite its limitations.

Exit counseling is a family-intervention process in which the family of a cult member, along with the cult member, participates in educational sessions. The family has as much responsibility to be educated about the issues of mind control and cult involvement as does the exit counseling team.

The approach taken here is one way to implement an intervention; it is *not* the only way. The important issue is the thoughtful and thorough preparation of the family that is necessary to undertake an intervention. Family members should work closely with their selected exit counselor(s) in order to determine the best approach for their situation. The goal of an exit counseling intervention is to help a loved one evaluate his or her involvement in a cultic group.

Carol Giambalvo
Flagler Beach, Florida

INTRODUCTION

In the mid-1970s increasing numbers of parents began to consult mental health professionals and clergy about their children's involvements in new religious groups that many called cults. Parents reported that formerly well-adjusted and engaged young adults (many were college students) changed radically, sometimes over a short period of time. These young adults typically dropped out of school, shunned their families and friends, and devoted themselves full time to working for these strange new groups to which they had pledged their total allegiance. Many parents concluded that their children had undergone a type of brainwashing.

Unfortunately for these parents, few helping professionals took their concerns seriously. Most assumed that these parents were overprotective or that their children were merely "going through a phase." But a handful of professionals, including Dr. John Clark on the East Coast and Dr. Margaret Singer on the West Coast, listened to the parents and began to speak out publicly. Soon, small and loosely organized groups of parents began to form in different parts of the country.

Several of these groups joined together to form the Citizens Freedom Foundation, later renamed the Cult Awareness Network (CAN). CAN became the leading grass-roots organization for this movement. One informal group in Massachusetts gave birth, so to speak, to the American Family Foundation (AFF), which has become the leading professional organization concerned with cults and psychological manipulation. Both AFF and CAN were chartered in 1979.

While these groups were developing, parents were doing what they could to rescue their children from what the parents considered very dangerous situations. Through trial and error the controversial process of "deprogramming" developed. In the 1970s, for many parents deprogramming became the preferred means of rescuing a cultist. Indeed, some parents mistakenly believed that no one left a cult unless he or she was deprogrammed.

Deprogramming was controversial because it involved forcing a cultist to listen to people relate information not available in the cults. Cultists were sometimes abducted from the street; although more commonly they were simply prevented from leaving their homes, a vacation cabin, a motel room, or whatever location was chosen for the deprogramming process. Even though deprogrammings usually succeeded in extricating the family member from the cult, they failed more often than many persons realized; and sometimes lawsuits were filed against parents and deprogrammers.

Deprogrammings were arranged through informal, quasi-underground means. Much secrecy surrounded the process for many years. Mental health professionals like myself were almost always "out of the loop"—in part because most of us did not want to become involved for ethical and legal reasons and in part because our expertise was to a large extent irrelevant to the deprogramming itself. Our main role was to help families cope with their alarm about a child or loved one in a cult and to help former cultists and their families cope with the many problems that accompanied reentry into mainstream society. However, sometimes mental health professionals or clergy were able to persuade those still in a cult to talk voluntarily about their cult involvements. Sometimes these conversations resulted in a decision to leave the cult.

Because of these successes, the legal risks entailed in deprogramming, and the ethical discomfort most parents and some deprogrammers felt, noncoercive means of helping cultists reevaluate their cult affiliations began to get more attention. By the mid-1980s it had become clear to many persons that what had come to be called exit counseling was at least as effective as deprogramming and certainly was much less risky—psychologically as well as legally. A few individuals committed themselves to doing exit counseling and refused to do "involuntaries."

Even within the exit counseling field, further branching off has occurred. Some exit counselors tend to be technique-oriented and/or advance a particular religious perspective. Others, such as Carol Giambalvo, are information-oriented. They present themselves as individuals with important information. Although they may have a preference regarding how the cultist chooses to respond to that information, they take pains to avoid manipulating the cultist. They simply present the information in an understandable format and at a pace that is comfortable for the cultist.

During the past few years some exit counselors have been trying to professionalize their field by establishing ethical and competency criteria. One step in this direction is that most exit counselors have agreed to the following statement of purpose:

> The purpose of exit counseling is to promote critical thinking skills especially regarding the use of mind control. Exit counselors will not violate clients' rights to self-determination nor will they unduly influence clients' ideological or spiritual orientation.

Although this process of professionalization had not reached closure at the time of writing, much progress has been made.

One of the most important achievements to date is this book, a revised second edition, in which Carol Giambalvo succinctly and clearly describes what an exit counseling involves. She gives families practical advice and hope and she relieves their anxiety by lifting the veil from a process that has been viewed with much more awe than it deserves.

Exit counseling is not mysterious. At heart it is simply respectful communication. In a way it is analogous to Radio Free Europe or the Voice of America transmitting information "through" the iron curtain to the people living in the closed societies of Eastern Europe and the former Soviet Union. There is no magic. There is merely the patient, persistent communication of that which ultimately shatters all walls: truth, honesty, respect, and love.

Michael D. Langone, Ph.D.
Executive Director, American Family Foundation
Editor, Cultic Studies Journal

1. PRE-INTERVENTION

Why Consult an Exit Counselor?

Helping a cultist reevaluate his or her commitment to a cult calls for specialized information, knowledge, experience, and skills. It also requires a certain amount of objectivity that most families do not have regarding the life of their loved one. For example, a parent, who is a physician, was consulting me about his son's cult involvement. He said he wanted an experienced exit counselor. Even though he had done considerable research into the cult in question, he used the analogy that he would not attempt to do surgery on his son. He realized that he lacked objectivity and the in-depth knowledge of mind control that exit counselors offered.

One of the first things a cult does is undermine the outside relationships of a new recruit. The primary attack is on the parents and family. For this reason, approaching the cultist armed with negative information about the cult, no matter how credible it seems, will not work. It's important to remember that because of the cultic pressures and manipulations on the cult member, his or her family has lost its credibility. Similarly, cults are known to attack the credibility of clergy, religions, and belief systems other than their own.

Exit counselors are usually former cult members themselves. They have firsthand experience with mind control. They have knowledge of cult mind-sets, the dynamics of cult membership, and the history of the particular cult in question and its leader(s). They also have the ability to bypass the closed thinking brought about by mind control in order to reaccess the cultist's critical thinking abilities. These are vital areas of expertise. Families often say that they want the best chance for their loved ones and that is why they choose to use a professional exit counselor.

How to Find and Evaluate Exit Counselors

Referrals to exit counselors can come through such organizations as the American Family Foundation (AFF) and the Cult Awareness Network (CAN), as well as the cult clinics and rehabilitation facilities listed in the back of this book. Often parents are referred to an exit counselor by a former member of their loved one's cult or by a family who has participated in a family intervention.

Before consulting an exit counselor, families should make sure that their reasons for doing so are valid. Sometimes cult-aware mental health professionals or clergy can help families clarify this issue. They can also provide information on exit counseling and exit counselors.

Families who decide to consult an exit counselor should take their time in the selection process; they should interview exit counselors. During the interview process, there are several factors to keep in mind. These can be evaluated by asking about and discussing the following:

- How will my family member relate to this person?

- Ask for the exit counselors' experience in interventions with the particular cult in question.

- Do the exit counselors seem knowledgeable about mind control and cults in general? Do they present this information clearly?

- Ask for fee structures and other expenses that may be involved.

- Ask for references from families for whom they have worked.

- •Ask for references from people in CAN or AFF and/or mental health professionals. Are they in good standing with these organizations?

- •Ask for approximate percentages of people they have worked with who ultimately left a cult.

- •Are they willing to spend the time needed to adequately prepare the family for the intervention?

Preparation of the Family

The family's initial contact with the exit counselors involves a lengthy conversation or series of conversations. During these discussions, the exit counselor needs to calm the family and take the panic out of the situation. This is particularly true if the family has just discovered that the group the loved one is involved with is a cult.

Preparation of the family is crucial to the success of a voluntary intervention. This preparation should not be omitted unless there is an extreme emergency. Family members need help in dealing with a range of emotions so that they are able to inform themselves about mind control, about cults in general, and about the particular group the cultist belongs to.

The following sections contain material that should be covered before setting up a family intervention.

What *Not* To Say or Do

- •Don't say, "You're in a cult. You're brainwashed."

- •Don't say, "You can't make any decisions for yourself."

•Don't argue with the cultist about the cult's beliefs.

•Don't criticize the group or the leaders.

•Don't be confrontational.

•Don't give large sums of money or relinquish trusts or bank accounts to cult members.

•Don't turn over titles or deeds to cult members.

What *To* Do

It is important to the progress of an intervention that the family keep open the lines of communication with the loved one. If the family is negative toward the group, the cultist becomes defensive and often feels personally attacked. Generally, this results in even further alienation of the cultist from family and friends. It is best that parents and other family members maintain a neutral position toward the group involvement.

Other suggested activities that can be important for relating to cultists are:

•Maintain an interest in their activities.

•Reaffirm your approval of their positive actions and motives, their good intentions, but do not approve of the group.

•Attend group activities or church with them, but don't go to retreats or long seminars.

- Negotiate with them: "I'll attend (church or Bible study or whatever) with you. Will you give me equal time in the future?"

- Take your time, educate all those who will be involved in the intervention, talk to other parents who have gone through this process, talk to former members.

Educating the Family about Cults

Family members must educate themselves on the issues of mind control, cults in general, and the specific cult their loved one has joined. The importance of this cannot be overemphasized. Families can contact the Cult Awareness Network (CAN) and the American Family Foundation (AFF) for information packets. Local CAN affiliates are available to offer support.

Consult the Bibliography at the end of this book for a list of books and articles. The most important materials are highlighted with an asterisk. Everyone who will be involved in the intervention should read the recommended material.

Through CAN or FOCUS (Former Cult Members' Support network), the family may be referred to former members of the group in question. If so, the family should ask former members about their experience in the group, why they left, if they were exit counseled, and, if so, what did their family say to them that caused them to be willing to listen and talk to the counselors.

Also through CAN or FOCUS, the family may ask for referrals to parents of former members, especially parents who prepared themselves well for an intervention. This will help calm the parents.

It is best to have a meeting with the exit counselor(s) before the intervention. If this is not possible, phone consultations can take place.

Information Gathering by Exit Counselors

During the initial contact with the inquiring parents or family, exit counselors need to gather the following preliminary information: name(s) of inquirers and relationship to cultist; name, age, and sex of cultist; name and location of the cult; length of time the cultist has been involved and extent of involvement (for example, whether or not he or she is in a leadership position).

The family is sent an extensive intake form to fill out and return. A summary of the exit counselor's fees and expenses is sent at this time.

Information from the family about the cultist's personal history, as well as family background, is crucial to help counselors understand the cultist, assess the procedure to be followed, and weigh the probable success of the intervention. Also it will help to determine particular areas of concern that the counselors need to identify—such as control issues between parents and cultist, possible hidden agendas of the parents or family, and special mental health issues.

A mental health professional should be consulted if certain areas of concern become obvious. These areas include, but are not limited to, serious defects in interpersonal skills, drug or alcohol abuse by the family or the cultist, prior emotional or mental breakdowns, dysfunctional family situations, physical problems (pregnancy, diabetes, any illness affected by emotional stress), prior eating disorders, self-destructive behavior or suicidal tendencies.

If there are concerns about the cultist's emotional ability to deal with an intervention, the family needs to consult a mental health professional who is knowledgeable about cult issues. In these cases, the family needs to get an opinion on the timing of an intervention and should ask the mental health professional to be available during the intervention. In a dysfunctional family situation, the family should be referred to a professional for pre-intervention counseling.

Note: If indications of dysfunctions such as those described above or other areas of concern regarding the cultist's state of mental health become evident during the intervention, a consultation with a mental health professional may be appropriate before proceeding with the intervention.

Logistical Factors

Once the family decides on a specific exit counselor to employ, details on logistical matters should be explored with that exit counselor.

Timing

Find a time when it would be natural for the cultist to visit home: family celebrations, holidays, birthdays, semester breaks, perhaps a family vacation.

Location

There are many variables regarding location. It is preferable to consult with the exit counselors concerning the best site for the intervention.

Team Composition

Generally, a team consists of two exit counselors. Sometimes a team of three is helpful, for example, in the case of multiple cultists or a cultist who is in a position of leadership.

One of the team should be a former member of the cult in question. If the cultist is in a Bible-based cult, one of the team members needs to have a knowledge of Scripture and be sensitive to the ethical issues involved.

It is preferable to have at least one member of the team be the same gender as the cultist.

The lead exit counselor should have the final say on the composition of the team.

Travel Arrangements

In most cases, the family makes the plane reservations, prepays the round-trip tickets, and arranges for either mail delivery or airport pick-up of the tickets. In the long run it is more economical to buy tickets without restrictions should the situation warrant last-minute changes. Some exit counselors prefer to make their own travel arrangements.

The family arranges for transportation from the airport to the team's lodgings. If the family is unable to pick up the team at the airport, arrangements for rental car, taxi, or other transportation can be discussed.

The entire team should arrive at least a full day before the intervention so there is time for the family to meet with all the team members. This is necessary for final planning and consultations.

Accommodations

Pre-intervention: Motel or hotel accommodations may be necessary for the team. If possible, team members can stay with relatives or friends of the family.

During intervention: Some exit counselors prefer to stay in the same location as the cultist and the family to be able to socialize with them when not working with the cultist and to be on hand should the client "float" (that is, go back into the cult mind-set) or have nightmares or other difficulties during the night.

If staying with the family is not possible, other accommodations should be arranged. If the cultist prefers that the team not stay with the family, this request should be respected.

Some exit counselors prefer to stay in separate accommodations to give the cultist and the family private time to interact. Consult with the lead exit counselor regarding his or her preference on this matter.

Meals

It is best if the team, cultist, and family can share meals and breaks so that they are able to socialize, relax, and interact together.

There may be special diet considerations and timing for meals. Consult with exit counselors about this. Snacks and beverages should be accessible during the sessions.

Breaks/Schedules

The cultist should have the most control over this area. The team needs to monitor the stress factor and the cultist's ability to absorb and assimilate the information presented. There needs to be sensitivity toward information overload. It helps the process to take frequent breaks.

Encourage the cultist to go for walks, to play a sport or games with family members, or to take a nap—to get away from the counselors for some time, if possible.

The more intense information requiring critical thinking should be reserved for mornings when everyone is fresh. During evening sessions, it is better to deal with lighter issues or to show videos.

Videos

Educational videotapes are used during an intervention. The family should be encouraged to watch the videos so that all the participants are educated. A VHS VCR will be needed for this purpose. A remote control is necessary so that the videotape can be paused for discussion.

During the showing of videos, remember to be sensitive: allow the cultist to "save face" with his or her family.

Length of Intervention

Usually an intervention lasts three to five days, sometimes longer. The length depends entirely on the cultist's willingness to deal with issues and his or her ability to relate to and integrate the information.

Family Matters

The Family Team

Personal confidentiality and sensitivity in planning the intervention are important. The family should tell no one other than those who need to know.

To ascertain the main players on the family team, consider the following:

- Who is important to the cultist and to the intervention?
- Who was closest to the cultist before his or her cult involvement?
- Who had or still has the most influence on the cultist?
- Which nonfamily members may have influence, such as teachers, clergy, family friends?

Only those who are particularly significant to the cultist should be called upon for the intervention.

Sometimes it is necessary to do a pre-intervention intervention with a family member who is unwilling to participate in the intervention or who does not understand the issues.

Family members should exercise caution not to reveal to the cultist how well-informed they are about the group. Doing so may result in the cult's taking measures to counteract the family's influence. For example, the cult may order the cult member not to visit his or her family.

Family Meeting with the Intervention Team

This meeting occurs the day or evening before the actual intervention. It takes place in the town where the intervention is to happen, usually somewhere nearby, such as in the motel or home where the exit counseling team is spending the night. It is important that all the steps previously outlined have been taken to educate all family members taking part in the intervention.

All team members and all family participants should be included in this pre-intervention session.

The purpose of this session is to reassure the family (especially if they have not met the team in person) and to address any anxieties and calm the family. It serves as an opportunity to provide the exit counselors with any additional pertinent information. It helps to ensure that family members will know how to talk to the cultist the following day in hopes that the cultist will be willing to work with the exit counselors.

Each family member should be given an opportunity to express his or her feelings about the intervention and to ask about areas of concern or his or her role in the intervention. It is the last chance to clear up any confusions or hesitations before meeting with the cultist.

At this meeting, each family member is asked for his or her expectation of how the cultist may respond to the intervention.

There should be some practice sessions for each family member to role-play what she or he will say to the cultist, while another family member plays the role of the cultist. Participants should be coached where necessary. As much as possible, families should use explanations and language that are consistent with the family style.

Possible Scenarios

Suggestions for Presenting the Plan to the Cultist

The following approaches have worked in exit counseling situations. Consider each one carefully while planning the best approach for your loved one.

- We've seen some changes in you since your involvement with ________. Some of these changes are very positive. Nevertheless, we've been concerned and we didn't know exactly why.

- We've tried to understand what is happening to you. We've even gone to some group events with you and what we saw concerned us even more. So we started looking further to try to understand our growing concern for your welfare. The more information we came across—and it took a long, hard search to find this information—the more our concerns for you grew because we don't think you have access to this information.

- It's been an extremely upsetting and anxiety-producing time for us—because as we educated ourselves, we became aware that if we presented this information to you, you would become defensive and want to withdraw from us. We were afraid we were going to lose you.

- We had to find a way to present this information to you and that seemed to us like interfering in your life and you're an adult. We had to think long and hard about intervening in your life because we've always trusted your ability to make decisions for yourself. Yet we felt certain that if you had access to the information we saw, you would want to reevaluate your commitment to the group. So, we have searched for some people who have experience with this group and we asked them to talk to you and to us so we *all* can understand the group and each other.

• We ask you just to talk with these people and hear all the information as objectively as you can. What you do with this information is entirely up to you—it is *your* decision. We know we can count on you to make a good decision for yourself. But we couldn't live with ourselves unless we made sure we were responsible enough to allow you the opportunity to make a *fully informed* decision. We will stand behind the decision you make after you have heard all the information.

• You have spent *x* amount of time with the group, we're asking you for three or four days.

• We asked you to talk with someone with us and you said you would. (*use only if this applies*)

• This time you spend will affect the rest of your life. You're changing your life goals around the group, so it is important that you know all there is to know and it is important to *us* as your family to know that it is *your* decision *alone*. So, we ask you to spend this time with these people without input from the group. Please don't make or receive any phone calls so we can be assured that this is *your* decision.

- It's a win/win situation. If you hear all they have to say and, in the end, you still think it is irrelevant to your involvement with the group, then you're affirmed in your commitment and you win. If you listen and see that you need to reevaluate your commitment, you also win. We're all given the opportunity to hear this information and to understand you better, so we *all* win.

- If your group has the truth, truth can always stand up to inspection.

Bear in mind that the exit counselors and the family are attempting to present reality to a person who is out of touch with reality—due to a complex combination of emotional, psychological, and social manipulation. These manipulations are part of cultic group dynamics, performed without the cultist's knowledge.

Remember, do not argue with the cultist. It will only trigger his or her cult mind-set. It is better to remain non-confrontational, nonjudgmental, and supportive. Let your warmth and concern shine through. The best point of view to take is to acknowledge that the intervention is about helping the *whole family*—and the cultist is an *integral* member of that whole.

Possible Interchanges with the Cultist

Cultist: What do these people know about my group? You have to experience the group to understand.

Possible response: They have experienced the group, let them tell you their stories.

Cultist: They're under Satan's influence. What church do they go to?

Possible response: They're not here to represent any church's perspective. They will deal with the Bible with you and look at your church's teachings about the Bible with you.

Cultist: You lied to me. You tricked me into being here. You set this whole thing up behind my back.

Possible response: We felt if we asked you to come look at this information, you would have asked advice from the group and you would have been advised not to do it. We feel like we're losing you—like we can't talk openly with you. It hurts us to do this, but what would you do if it were your son or daughter? We would do the same if you had a drug or alcohol problem and we feel that's the extent of your jeopardy.

We have proof that your group has not been up-front with you either, but there was no way to deal with that without doing it this way. We're doing this so we can break the rule of silence and begin to talk with one another openly again. We're sorry it had to be this way, but we couldn't take a chance any other way.

We love you. We have tried our best to do what is best for you and for all of us, under the circumstances. Try to think of it this way: we've gone to much effort and have had to make a very difficult ethical decision to try to help you—out of our love for you.

What to Expect During the Intervention

Some things the family may see happening during the intervention:

Vacillation: It may appear that some progress is being made. Then following a nap or after a night's sleep, it seems like the cultist is back to the first step again.

Anger: It is focused at the family or at the situation. Anger is usually expressed in body language, but sometimes it is expressed verbally or physically.

The Stages of an Intervention: (These don't always follow a progression; the person may vacillate.)

•Denial
•Resistance
•Interest
•Participation

Options for Presenting the Plan to the Cultist

There are two options for presenting a voluntary family intervention to the cultist:

1) The family presents the plan to the cultist and obtains consent. The family then brings in the team;

2) The team (or part of the team) is present to help the family members when they talk to the cultist.

The first option is the better one because the cultist feels more like she or he has control.

Since cults are doing more and more training and preparation to work against deprogramming, often it is helpful for an exit counselor to be present to assure the cultist that he or she will be free to leave when desired and that no one is present with the intention of taking the cultist away from his or her faith (or of taking away his or her transformation, in the case of a New Age group). The cultist is assured that the exit counselors are present simply to explore some information together.

The family members should decide which option is best, based on how comfortable they are with the information and how they think the cultist will respond. The exit counselors may advise that one option is better than the other, depending on the family situation and the experience they have had with the specific cult in question.

The exit counselors should advise the family on the extent of involvement of specific family members and/or friends in the *family* part of the intervention (that is, when the family tries to convince the cultist to speak with the exit counselors). The more loving, open, and honest the cultist's relationship is with a parent, loved one, or family member, the more that person should be involved.

If any relationship between the cultist and another family member is problematic, it may be best for the other person to be less involved. He or she can show support simply by being present. Occasionally it is preferable that the person not be there at all. A similar assessment should be made of all siblings, family members, and friends.

Post-Cult Counseling

A growing body of research indicates that a cult's environmental pressures and psychological manipulations cause people to experience considerable psychological distress when they leave their group. Therefore, it is advisable that former cultists seriously think about getting professional psychological assistance during their recovery period and transition into mainstream society.

Some ex-cultists may require only a few hours of consultation to help clarify their needs and identify a strategy for coping with the problems they are likely to encounter. Others may require psychotherapy. Some may need a period of "rehabilitation" at a live-in facility. The American Family Foundation can provide a list of mental health professionals with some knowledge of cults (see Resources at the end of this book).

Because the demands of day-to-day living can consume so much time, few ex-cultists pay as much attention as they should to their post-cult psychological needs. Therefore, even for those whose problems are not severe, a strategic "retreat" from the pressures of practical life can greatly facilitate a smooth transition.

Rehab/Reentry Facilities

Not every ex-cultist *needs* to go to a reentry facility. Those who are able to, however, seem to recover from their cult experience at a faster rate and with less difficulty than those who do not. At present, there are two rehab/reentry facilities available in the United States.

Rehab facilities offer an opportunity to take time away from the pressures of immediate changes in the life of an exiting cult member—changes in school, job, and living arrangements. Here ex-cultists are given the time to relax, to continue to educate themselves about undue influence and mind control, and to further integrate the information they received during the intervention.

Also, the ex-cultist may have issues about the intervention, his or her family, or pre-cult matters that were unresolved before cult involvement. These issues are likely to surface at this time. Rehab facilities are an excellent place to sort through these concerns with professional help and begin to resolve them.

Having been involved in a cult and under the influence of mind control is a serious situation. The family may need to evaluate the ex-cultist's job or school schedule. In some cases, the family may want to consider whether the ex-cultist would be better off leaving school for a semester. This may be necessary, in particular, if she or he had been deeply involved in the group.

Even though interventions give the ex-cultist tools for recovery, leaving a cult is a traumatic event in a person's life. Its seriousness should not be minimized. The ex-cultist will be going through an intense identity crisis as well as a period of grief. For these reasons, attending a rehabilitation facility is highly recommended, if it is at all feasible.

Families can contact facilities directly to evaluate their services. See the Resources section at the back of this book for the names and locations of the rehab facilities.

Future plans

Former cultists who seek professional psychological assistance or attend a rehab/reentry facility will devote considerable time to thinking about future plans. Those who don't seek help must also address this issue at some point. Families should try not to pressure the ex-cultist.

Below are listed some important concerns that family and friends can help the ex-cultist identify and think about.

(1) Is he or she living with other group members? How can the family help the ex-cultist move out, retrieve belongings, and deal with the other members?

(2) Is he or she employed by the cult or are there other members of the cult at the workplace? Will the ex-cultist need some financial support before she or he becomes reemployed or financially independent?

(3) Has the former cultist chosen the school he or she is attending because the cult wanted recruitment done on that particular campus? He or she may want to transfer schools. There may be a loss of tuition or school time.

(4) Is there a need for long-term counseling or therapy with a mental health professional?

(5) Are there FOCUS contacts or a support group in the area? Provide the ex-cultist with a list of such contacts.

(6) Does the ex-cultist have family support? This is extremely important: the cultist needs to have something to come out *to*.

2. THE INTERVENTION

The Author's Philosophy

The author's family interventions are based on an educational model. The cultist has been a victim of a sophisticated set of manipulations. Once she or he becomes aware of these manipulations, basic integrity usually will not allow the cultist to remain a part of a system that victimizes others—no matter how lofty the goals. An intervention, for the most part, is a discourse on ethics, values, and integrity.

The material is to be presented in a manner that shows respect for the cultist's dignity. In particular, it is important to be sensitive to the emotional trauma the cultist may undergo while confronting these issues. Material is to be put forth at a pace that allows the cultist to assimilate the information and, simultaneously, deal with its emotional impact.

The goal is for the cultist to reevaluate his or her commitment to the group. Although parents and exit counselors may hope that he or she chooses to leave, leaving is not the goal. *Informed* choice is the goal.

It is important that the cultist leave the group with dignity and self-respect intact. There are some positive aspects to a person's cult involvement. Encourage the cultist to be patient, to sort out the positives from the negatives, and to integrate the positives into their present and future life.

Once a person understands mind control techniques, that person has the basic tools with which to sort out these issues and deal with them. This process takes time. But there is much less time involved and much less stress on the individual if she or he has had the opportunity for exit counseling and rehabilitation. It is imperative that the family understand this whole process so they can be supportive to the cultist.

The Intervention Begins

Introductions

At this point, it is assumed that the family has been successful in getting the cultist to engage with the exit counselors. Now the exit counseling team should be introduced to the cultist. Once the cultist agrees to speak with the exit counselors, she or he then becomes their "client," that is, the person whose welfare is the paramount concern of the exit counselors.

All the members of the exit counseling team should let the client know their names, where they are from, and their experience with the group in question.

During the initial "getting-acquainted" session, it should be made clear to the client that the purpose is not to take the individual away from his or her beliefs or faith in God (or, in the case of membership in a New Age group, from his or her transformation)—no one can do that. Tell the client that there are many good things he or she has learned about him- or herself, such as how to relate to others. Point out there have been some good effects on his or her life while a member of the group. Go on to say that there are many truths found in this group, and probably it is the people and the "truth" found in the group that attracted the client to the group.

These facts need to be stated in the beginning because much of the information to be gone over in the ensuing sessions may seem negative.

It should also be stated at this time that the purpose of the process is to explore information together, not to argue or debate. The goal is to provide information that will enable the client to make a fully informed choice—the exit counselors are on the client's side. The information will speak for itself and will be well documented.

Sorting Out the Issues

During this stage, exit counselors try to elicit the following information from the client:

- Where and how did the client join the group?
- What attracted him or her to the group?
- What does the client find positive about participating in the group?
- Has the client had some questions or serious doubts about the group? If so, how were those issues addressed by the group and leaders?
- What were the client's life goals before meeting the group? What are they presently? (Often here it becomes obvious that the goals have changed.)
- If goals have changed, can the client identify why, how, and when they changed, or if she or he was even aware that they had changed?
- When the client first met the group, what did she or he think the group was about? Has that changed?
- When he or she first met the group, what were his or her expectations of the group? Are those initial expectations being met, or has the client found it necessary to change those expectations?

Through the process of these exchanges, most often counselors can assess the area that has the client "hooked" into the group—emotionally or intellectually. Generally it is some of both, but one area tends to have a stronger influence. This assessment will determine which issues will need to be dealt with first.

In an exit counseling situation, the word *doctrine* refers to the beliefs and practices of the group. While the particular beliefs of a group are not at issue in an intervention, they must be addressed because the practices and techniques that are employed get twisted around the beliefs. The beliefs or doctrine are usually what "justify" the use of techniques of emotional and social manipulation.

The client's positive motivations (wanting to do what God wants, wanting to change the world for the better) and good intentions are acknowledged and respected. The client's integrity is most important. Also the client's sincerity is valued, as is the sincerity of those in the group. Sincerity and good motives are not being called into question.

The issue that does get addressed is the process by which a person's sincere desires may be channeled into something quite different, one step at a time, without the awareness of the individual. Examples are given that point to the sincerity of members of other cults, illustrating how those people are manipulated. Methods of manipulation—social, emotional, and psychological—are discussed at length and in detail so the client can begin to recognize what may apply to his or her experience.

This will lead into discussing the fact that many critics of the group have accused it of being a cult and using mind control, which, of course, the group denies. Since this accusation has been made, the client is asked, "Don't you think it's important to look at what a cult is and why people use the word to describe your group? What is mind control? We need to look at this carefully so you can decide for yourself whether it is present in your group."

At this point in the intervention the client may flatly deny the problem. The client may even say that these issues are not important anyway because "I know this group has the truth." If this happens, it is appropriate to ask whether the client is really saying "the ends justify the means." Does truth really need certain techniques to get people to accept it? This focus should be dropped if the client becomes defensive.

If the client says that this particular issue is unimportant, then ask what information *she* or *he* thinks *is* important to explore at this time. The client should be asked what information would be important enough to cause a person to reevaluate his or her involvement? Usually a member of a Bible-based group will want to address doctrine, saying something like, "Show me where we're not going by the Bible."

Doctrinal problems (both beliefs and practices) can now be explored in an effort to engage the client's interest. The exit counselor should weave into this discussion how mind control methods get wrapped up in the doctrine because the leaders need the scriptures to justify their methodology. Here the exit counselor explains the difference between exegesis and eisegesis (the drawing out of a text one's theology versus the interpretation of a text by reading into it one's own ideas).

It should be pointed out that now it is important to begin to address mind control so the client can better see for him- or herself how these methods get wrapped up in the group's doctrine and how they become justifiable. It's like putting together the pieces of a puzzle so one can see the whole picture. First one has to be able to see each piece of the puzzle.

The models of mind control are discussed, with a brief description of whose models they are and who the experts are: Dr. Margaret T. Singer and Dr. Robert Jay Lifton. It is best to start with Dr. Margaret Singer's model because at this point her model is easier to understand.

Dr. Margaret T. Singer's Model: The Conditions for Mind Control

Dr. Singer points out that there are six conditions for mind control:

(1) Gaining control over a person's time, especially his or her *thinking* time.

(2) Creating a sense of powerlessness in the recruit, while providing models that demonstrate the new behavior that management (leadership) wants to produce.

(3) Manipulating rewards, punishments, and experiences in order to suppress the former social behavior of the recruit. Use of altered states of consciousness to manipulate experience.

(4) Manipulating rewards, punishments, and experiences in order to elicit the behavior that management (leadership) wants.

(5) Creating a tightly controlled system wherein those who dissent are made to feel as though there is something inherently wrong with them to be questioning.

(6) Keeping recruits unaware and uninformed. Management (leadership) cannot carry out a thought reform program with a person's full capacity and informed consent.

Often, at this stage, a videotape is shown of Dr. Singer addressing the Coercive Persuasion conference in 1988. Whenever videos are shown, they are paused to highlight an important issue. Each point is discussed at length, explaining how a particular technique is used in other cults, while drawing close parallels to how the client's cult uses it.

The Intervention Continues: The First Day

At this time, doctrinal areas that were discussed previously can be reviewed and applied to Dr. Singer's model. Also discussed are the differences between mind control and brainwashing and how the terms are often used interchangeably, even by experts. The author of this volume prefers the terms *mind control, coercive persuasion,* or *undue influence.*

By means of this discussion, exit counselors can demonstrate that they don't necessarily agree with everything the "experts" say. Exit counselors can state that they, too, have done some work on the matter and have come to their own conclusions. Basically, they want to put forth a model of critical thinking for the client. Remember, the team should be able to express some differences of opinion and should not demonstrate groupthink to the client.

A Video: *The Wave*

A video called *The Wave* is shown early on. It describes a true story about a high school teacher who indoctrinates his social studies class, and ultimately most of the high school, by conducting an experiment in mind control.

This important video usually is shown on the first day of an intervention because it demonstrates in a nonthreatening way how groups use mind control techniques. Generally Dr. Singer's model is presented before showing the video, thereby providing a basis for understanding the concept of mind control. The video is paused to interweave Dr. Singer's criteria with the video's story. If a point from Dr. Lifton's theories is obvious, then his model of mind control is introduced briefly.

It's a good idea for the exit counselors to have a discussion on any reactions to or questions about *The Wave*. They should try to get the client to discuss how it applies to the group in question, asking if she or he could see any similarities. Rarely is the client willing to come up with any at this point, but it's important to see his or her response to the question. By now, the client has probably had enough for the first day.

At this point, the exit counselors usually ask the client if he or she would like to call it a day. The client should always be asked how she or he is feeling. The flow of information should follow the pacing preferred by the client, unless the team is not up to it in some way.

Sometimes exit counselors need to pick up on body language. Be aware if a client is overloaded or tired, or if she or he is dissociating. Before retiring, the client should be asked what time she or he would like to begin the next morning. Negotiate the starting time, if necessary.

Other Areas Covered During the Intervention

The areas outlined below should be covered during the intervention. Depending on the group in question, there may be other pertinent information to go over, while certain other topics may not be discussed as thoroughly.

The order of topics varies in response to the client's desires or expressed interest.

•*Moonchild* (a video): A good example of Unification Church indoctrination. It is nonthreatening and a good lead-in to Dr. Lifton's criteria.

•Dr. Robert Jay Lifton's criteria: This should be discussed at length, citing examples of the ways in which the group in question uses the criteria.

1. Milieu control
2. Mystical manipulation
3. Demand for purity
4. Confession
5. Sacred science
6. Loading the language
7. Doctrine over person
8. Dispensing of existence

•The history of the group and the leader(s)

•Issues of deception and how this group uses it

•Cognitive dissonance

•Behavior modification/control

•Information control

•Phobia indoctrination

•Thought-stopping techniques

•Trances/altered states of consciousness; vulnerability to suggestion

- •Hypnosis: what is hypnosis (in depth)
  - ■Videos on hypnosis
  - ■*Captive Minds* video
- •Other videos: The use of videos depends upon the type of group. If the client processes information more easily through videos and discussion, this medium can be relied upon more heavily.
  - ■Videos of testimonies and panel discussions by former members
  - ■*Thy Will Be Done*

Even if a client indicates in some way that he or she is not returning to the group, the preceding information still needs to be covered to ensure that the client begins to understand his or her experience. The client will need these tools to unravel the ideas and behavior that she or he accepted while in the group due to the influence of mind control. This process is important to the client's recovery from the cult experience.

Things to Remember

An intervention usually lasts from three to five days, depending on the client's ability to process the information. It is important to direct questions at the client regularly to make sure she or he understands the information.

Remember, the client needs time to assimilate the information, reestablish relationships with the family, and allow his or her "former identity" to resurface. Along with this, he or she must deal with all the related emotions.

No one can really set a schedule for how this will transpire. Each client is different.

Documentation of Primary Sources

When exit counselors are covering practices and teachings of the group, they should see that these teachings are documented. Use the cult's literature, books, letters, audiotapes, and so forth. The client needs to see that the team has done its homework; it will be apparent that extensive research has allowed the team to document each point that is being made.

When referencing the group's audiotapes, it is best to use transcripts of the tapes to prevent the client from dissociating and/or "floating" at the sound of the leader's voice. The actual audiotapes should be available, however, in case the client wants to verify the transcripts' authenticity.

Family Attendance

It is important for the intervention team to watch for signs of floating (dissociation), fatigue, or information overload, all the while monitoring the client's emotional well-being.

Exit counselors need to be sensitive to the client's potential embarrassment over some (or all) issues when the family is present. At times, it is preferable to have most family members leave once the team begins to address deeper issues. In some cases, the client may want the whole family to participate in the entire intervention. But most importantly, those times when the client wants to speak in privacy to the counselors must be respected.

Usually the client's parents remain in the house the entire time to help with meals, errands, snacks, and so forth. At least one family member should always be present in the house in case the client indicates a desire to terminate the intervention.

Closing Issues

If the client decides to leave the group, the parents should be on guard against creating a watchful atmosphere, known as the fish-bowl effect. Parents need to resist their natural instincts to pull the ex-cultist back under their wings. Instead, they need to give their loved one his or her wings. Parents should be there for the ex-cultist when needed, and they should not be afraid of every phone call from a cult member.

The intervention gives the client an educational experience. The usual outcome is for the client to remain wary of any group for some time to come.

Both parents and client should be told about two helpful resources:

(1) *Influence*, by Dr. Robert Cialdini, a book available from the Cult Awareness Network; and

(2) *Recovery from Cults*, edited by Dr. Michael Langone, a comprehensive book that provides guidelines for ex-cultists, families, and professionals (to become available in 1993).

For further information on these resources, consult the Bibliography at the end of this book.

What to Do When the Client Decides to Return to the Cult

If the client decides to return to the group, the exit counselors should cover the following points, if appropriate:

(1) Remind the client that the purpose of the intervention was twofold: [a] it provided information not readily

available to him or her through the group; and [b] the client was educated about mind control and undue influence. The exit counselors should reinforce the good intentions and motivations of the family, underlining the fact that everything is now out in the open. Always encourage future communication.

(2) Prepare the client for the likelihood that for a short time the group may hold him or her up as a hero, but also the group may distort what actually happened in the intervention. The exit counselors should ask the client to remember what *actually* happened and the way he or she was actually treated. Remind the client of the importance of keeping his or her own integrity intact.

(3) Reinforce the idea that the client now knows what mind control is and will be aware of it in the future.

(4) Role-play with the client how she or he thinks the leaders will handle the return to the group and how she or he will respond to their questions about why they weren't called for advice when the client was faced with the intervention. The exit counselors can have the client play the leader's role, then his or her own.

When the Client Decides to Leave the Cult

If the client leaves the group, the following areas may be important to address, depending on the needs of the client:

- How to help friends to get out.

- Whether or not to talk to leadership.

- How to move out of the group house.

- How to handle feelings of embarrassment.

- How to deal with the temporary loss of the power of concentration, a common post-cult problem. (Exit counselors can suggest using the electronic game, Simon, to help restore concentration and help with short-term memory loss.)

- What to say to friends not in the group and how to rebuild relationships outside the group.

- What is the value of counseling and rehabilitation facilities. (These should be strongly encouraged).

- What are the role and potential value of FOCUS support groups, individual contacts for support, and conferences on issues of cult recovery.

- How to recognize and deal with residuals and floating. What is it and how long does it last? How to help oneself deal with it, including identifying "triggers."

- What to do about spirituality. (If the client will be going to a rehab/reentry facility, this issue should be addressed there rather than with exit counselors.)

When the client raises issues and concerns such as those described above or asks counselors for advice, it is important for the exit counselors *not to advise the client; rather they should merely explore options with the client.*

Exit counselors should always keep in mind the extreme vulnerability of those who have just left cultic groups and mind control environments. It takes some time to relearn how to make decisions for oneself, especially when a person has been dependent on a group or leaders. Foster independent decision making from the very beginning. Explore this important matter with parents and family as well.

Under no circumstances should an exit counselor influence a client in any particular direction about his or her religious practice or faith or any other beliefs. In all these areas it is best to only *explore options* with the client. One option, however, is for the client to talk to clergy about specific religious issues. The client need not be left hanging with regard to religion. But, in my view, the exit counselor should not proselytize or evangelize the client.

Wrap-up Talk

At the end of an intervention, sometimes it is appropriate to make a personal recounting of what just happened. A brief summation, similar to the one that follows, may be helpful in certain situations.

> Sometimes we hear the phrase, "I was deprogrammed," or "I was exit counseled." I'd like to address that for a minute to let you know how I feel about it. It's important to me that you know that I don't think anyone did anything *to* you these last few days—except to provide you with additional information. When you joined the group, you made the best decision you could have made *given the information you received at the time.* Now, your family simply

gave you the opportunity to receive some new information and with that you've reevaluated your initial decision based on full and complete information.

So, in the future, if you ever feel embarrassed about being in a cult, remember that you left the group because you made a good decision, a decision based on your integrity. Remember this, especially if and when you hear that the group says you left because you're sinning or because of something negative about you. That hurts. Remember, they have to say those things to justify the existence of the group and their continued membership in it. You just remember *your* reasons for leaving are good ones.

3. POST-INTERVENTION

Post-Intervention Precautions

The exit counselors' involvement with the ex-cultist will diminish as the intervention comes to a close and the client begins to make plans for the future.

However, it is important to recognize that one of the residuals from a cultic experience is that ex-cultists are in the habit of having someone else advise them and make decisions for them. Sometimes a client transfers the loyalty he or she felt toward other cult members and cult leaders to an exit counselor or another member of the intervention team. Often following an intervention there are mutual feelings of affection between the client and exit counselors because of the amount of time spent together, the intensity of the counseling situation, and the gratitude felt toward the exit counselors.

Exit counselors must be sensitive to these residual effects and to the client's feelings. They should be especially careful not to promote any transference of loyalty from the cult leaders to themselves.

Some Options for the Ex-Cultist

Rehab/Reentry

If the client goes to a rehab facility, it may be necessary for a member of the intervention team to accompany him or her. This serves two purposes: (1) it will ease the transition; and (2) the team member can inform the facility staff of any issues the exit counselors feel the client needs to address. Also the exit counselor can let the staff know if the client is experiencing any episodes of floating.

If a member of the team does not accompany the client, the lead exit counselor should speak with the director of the facility to give some insight into the client and the particular circumstances.

The exit counselors should contact the client at least once during his or her stay at the rehab facility, and once again following rehab to touch base and let the client know they care. Any further contact should be initiated by the client, unless he or she indicates the desire to work as a former member on future interventions.

Working on Intervention Teams

Some ex-cultists make the decision to work with exit counselors on intervention teams, serving as the former member who can speak directly from experience with a cultist about involvement in a cultic group.

It is recommended that this not be done for at least six months after leaving a group so the client has time to put things into perspective and sort out major life issues. Working on an intervention too soon can cause the client to be "triggered" and may be upsetting.

Being on an intervention team at a later time, however, can aid the healing process. The client has a sense of helping others get out of the group. Also this work may relieve leftover guilt feelings about the people the client recruited into the group when she or he was involved.

In addition, it serves to freshen the client's memory of why she or he left the cult. While working on an intervention team, the former member is asked to explain directly to the new client/cultist his or her reasons for leaving the group. This process makes it concrete for the ex-member on the team. Often former clients say that they gained new insights that they were unable to grasp during their own intervention because there was so much to deal with at the time.

Helping on others' cases can be very healthy for former members. Nevertheless, doing so needs to be approached in a balanced way, making sure the timing is right. The former member should already have made a healthy adjustment to his or her post-cult situation.

Ongoing Therapy or Counseling

Some clients may have issues that were present before joining the cult and these may resurface after leaving the group. Or they may have problems that arose during cult involvement that were not treated properly. For example, a client might have been experiencing addictive behavior, anxiety, or depression before cult involvement. A client might have been dysfunctional due to illness, divorce, death in the family, or addictive behavior of a parent. Often such issues can be exacerbated in a cultic environment.

Clients with difficulties should be encouraged to engage in ongoing therapy following the intervention and/or the time spent at a rehab facility. When possible, refer them to appropriate resources.

At all times exit counselors must keep in mind that they are not mental health professionals. When in doubt in any situation, refer the client and/or family to mental health professionals. Having access to mental health professionals with a knowledge of cults and mind control issues is, of course, the best situation.

RESOURCES

Organizations

American Family Foundation (AFF)
P.O. Box 2265
Bonita Springs, FL 33959
Tel: (212) 249-7693

Cult Awareness Network (CAN)
2421 W. Pratt Blvd., Suite 1173
Chicago, IL 60645
Tel: (312) 267-7777

FOCUS (Former Cult Members' Support network)
c/o CAN
2421 W. Pratt Blvd., Suite 1173
Chicago, IL 60645
Tel: (312) 267-7777

Counseling Services

Cult Clinic & Hotline
Jewish Board of Family & Children's Services
120 W. 57th Street
New York, NY 10019
Tel: (212) 632-4640

Cult Clinic
Jewish Family Service
6505 Wilshire Blvd., 6th fl.
Los Angeles, CA 90048
Tel: (213) 852-1234

Rehab Facilities

Cook Home
Enid, OK
Betty and Jack Cook
Tel: (405) 446-5406

Wellspring Retreat & Resource Center
Albany, OH
Dr. Paul Martin and Barbara Martin
Tel: (614) 594-8296

BIBLIOGRAPHY

The articles and books listed here can help families and former cultists who are seeking to advance their understanding of the cult phenomenon. Those resources highlighted with an asterisk (*) are highly recommended for families considering exit counseling. Books available through the Cult Awareness Network have "(CAN)" at the end of the listing. Books with specific ordering information or books available from the American Family Foundation have "(AFF)" at the end of the listing.

Books

Churches That Abuse. Ronald Enroth, Ph.D. (Zondervan, 1992.) Written by an evangelical sociologist, this book clearly demonstrates, through the use of detailed case studies, how religious groups, even when their doctrines appear to be sound, can harm their members through manipulative techniques of persuasion and control. This book is strongly recommended for families and ex-cultists affected by cultic Bible-based groups. (AFF)

* *Combatting Cult Mind Control*. Steven Hassan. (Park Street Press, 1988.) A former member of a destructive cult, Hassan provides an inside view of cult life, its abuses, and deep psychological disturbances and personality changes that it can cause. This book is especially helpful to families and former members. (CAN)

* *Cults and Consequences: The Definitive Handbook.* Edited by Rachel Andres and James R. Lane. (Commission on Cults and Missionaries of the Jewish Federation Council of Greater Los Angeles, 1988.) Nearly forty authors have contributed to this outstanding guide for anyone concerned with cults. The cult problem is examined from such a wide variety of vantage points that the reader cannot help but come away with a better understanding of cults. (CAN\AFF)

Cults in America: Programmed for Paradise. Willa Appel. (Holt, Rinehart & Winston, 1983.) This book helps dispel the myths and confusion surrounding cults. It explains the conversion process and how conversion is maintained over time with mind control techniques. The author also describes the changes that take place in persons in such an environment. (CAN)

Cults, Sects and the New Age. Rev. James J. LeBar. (Our Sunday Visitor Press, 1989.) For those seeking a perspective on the cult issue, this book should definitely be read. It is especially useful for Catholics. In the book, the Reverend James LeBar provides not only useful facts about cultic movements, but also he outlines excellent suggestions for working with cult victims. (CAN\AFF)

* *Cults: What Parents Should Know.* Joan Carol Ross, Ed.M., and Michael D. Langone, Ph.D. (Carol Publishing Group, 1989.) The authors present a detailed study on virtually every aspect of cult involvement. This is a practical guide to help parents with children in destructive groups. (AFF\CAN)

* *Deprogramming: A Case Study.* Steve Dubrow-Eichel, Ph.D. (Special issue of the *Cultic Studies Journal,* Vol.

6, No. 2, 1989.) Based on Dubrow-Eichel's doctoral dissertation at the University of Pennsylvania, this volume describes in detail the deprogramming of a Hare Krishna follower. Although the approach of the deprogrammer is very different from the exit counseling approach described in this book, the volume contains many insights into the process through which cultists come to leave their groups. (AFF)

The Discipling Dilemma. Edited by Flavil R. Yeakley, Jr. (Gospel Advocate Co., 1988.) This is a serious and well-documented study that analyzes the discipling movement in general and the Boston Church of Christ in particular. During his investigation of the Boston movement, the author was given an opportunity to administer personality tests to members of the Boston Church, as well as to members of other cultic groups and mainstream denominations. The results of these findings show the unhealthy personality changes taking place in the lives of cult members. (CAN)

* *Influence: The New Psychology of Modern Persuasion.* Robert B. Cialdini, Ph.D. (William Morrow, 1984.) Using results of a 15-year scientific investigation of the persuasion process, Cialdini illustrates that anyone who understands how natural human behavior patterns work can exploit others. The book contains practical advice on how to think critically about many everyday situations, including cult recruiting. (CAN)

Prison or Paradise? The New Religious Cults. A. James Rudin and Marcia R. Rudin. (Fortress Press, 1980.) This book describes in detail the growing cult phenomenon. The authors carefully review the histories, beliefs, recruiting methods, and daily lives of members of the major cults. It offers specific methods for countering the cults. (AFF)

Psychodynamic Perspectives on Religion, Sect, and Cult. Edited by David Halperin, M.D. (John Wright PSG Inc., 1983.) This is a scholarly book with chapters on many aspects of the cult problem. An important chapter is "The Role of Family Therapy in the Treatment of Symptoms Associated with Cult Affiliation" by Arnold Markowitz, M.S.W., Director of the Cult Clinic and Hotline of the New York Jewish Board of Family and Children's Services. (AFF)

Smashing the Idols: A Jewish Inquiry into the Cult Phenomenon. Edited by Gary D. Eisenberg. (Jason Aronson, Inc., 1988.) This Jewish Book Club selection reprints a wide variety of articles on issues of concern to non-Jewish readers—such as treatment issues—as well as articles on specifically Jewish concerns. (AFF)

Thought Reform and the Psychology of Totalism. Robert Jay Lifton, M.D. (University of North Carolina Press, 1989.) This classic study on thought reform offers an analysis of the experiences of fifteen Chinese citizens and twenty-five Westerners who underwent "brainwashing" by the Communist Chinese government. Of particular interest is chapter 22, which lists Lifton's eight psychological themes that constitute thought reform or a mind control program. These criteria have become the standard by which to determine whether mind control is present in a group. (CAN)

TM and Cult Mania. M.A. Persinger, Ph.D., N.J. Carey, M.D., and L.A. Suess, H.B.A. (Christopher Publishing, 1980.) In this in-depth investigation into the claims of

Transcendental Meditation (TM), the authors identify the psychological and social procedures used by TM and other cults to manipulate human behavior. These include suggestion, placebo reactions, simple relaxation, and the mislabeling of vague emotional experiences. This is a useful book for those involved with the human potential or New Age movements. (CAN)

Unholy Devotion. Harold L. Bussell, D.Min. (Zondervan, 1983.) This book examines the commonalities shared by cultists and Evangelical Christians. Dr. Bussell disdains the traditional evangelical approach to cults—the examination of heretical doctrines—and warns of the cultic tendencies that can be found in "born again" churches. The author criticizes an overemphasis on subjective religious experience, spiritualization of issues to justify actions, a high evaluation of leaders who use emotionalism, and not teaching young people to think critically. (CAN)

Articles

"Attacks on Peripheral versus Central Elements of Self and the Impact of Thought Reforming Techniques." Richard Ofshe and Margaret T. Singer. (*Cultic Studies Journal*, Vol. 3, No. 1, 1986.) An excellent comparison of the sophisticated mind control techniques used by contemporary cults and the techniques used by "first generation of interest" programs, such as the brainwashing methods used on prisoners of war and in political reeducation programs. (AFF)

"The Cult Clinic Helps Families in Crisis." Marsha Emmer Addis, et al. (*Social Casework: The Journal of Contem-*

porary Social Work, 1984.) This article describes the work of the cult clinic of the Jewish Family Service of Los Angeles. (AFF)

"Cult Formation." Robert Jay Lifton, M.D. (*The Harvard Mental Health Letter*, February 1991.) In this article, Lifton gives a synopsis of the eight psychological themes he finds present in ideological totalism and the serious psychological concerns this raises. (AFF)

* "Cult Involvement: Suggestions for Concerned Parents and Professionals." Michael D. Langone, Ph.D. (*Cultic Studies Journal*, Vol. 2, No. 1, 1985.) The author provides concrete suggestions for communicating with cultists and devising an ethical strategy for helping them reevaluate destructive group involvement. (AFF)

"Cults." Edited by John Hochman, M.D. (Special issue of *Psychiatric Annals: The Journal of Continuing Psychiatric Education*, April 1990.) Contributors discuss the phenomenology of cults, their history, their present form, and their psychiatric implications. Articles include "Thought Reform Programs and the Production of Psychiatric Casualties" by Drs. Margaret Singer and Richard Ofshe and "Working with Cult-Affected Families" by Dr. Michael Langone. (AFF)

* "Family Responses to a Young Adult's Cult Membership and Return." Lorna Goldberg, M.S.W., and William Goldberg, M.S.W. (*Cultic Studies Journal*, Vol. 6, No. 1, 1989.) The authors describe the different ways in which parents respond to a child's cult involvement. This article can help parents better understand *their* reactions. (AFF)

"'Reject the Wicked Man'—Coercive Persuasion and Deviance Production: A Study of Conflict Management." Jerry Paul McDonald. *(Cultic Studies Journal*, Vol. 5, No. 1, 1988.) A rather difficult but rich article written by a sociologist who spent ten years as a member of a Bible-based group. The author has many original insights into the techniques used to control cult members. (AFF)

"The Utilization of Hypnotic Techniques in Religious Cult Conversion." Jesse S. Miller, Ph.D. (*Cultic Studies Journal*, Vol 3, No. 2, 1986.) This article dispels the myths of "instant hypnosis" often used to describe cultic conversion and details the use of unannounced hypnotic trances. The latter are induced without a formal trance induction and without the permission or knowledge of the person being converted. (AFF)

Packets

In addition to many of the books and articles listed above, the American Family Foundation and the Cult Awareness Network make available packets of newspaper and magazine articles dealing with various groups.

* * * * *

Current publications of the American Family Foundation, along with ordering information, are listed in the following pages.

Selected Publications on Cultism and Psychological Manipulation

The following publications are available from the American Family Foundation. The suggested donation for each item, noted at the end of the listing, covers the costs of production, postage, and handling and contributes to the further development and distribution of education material by AFF. All payments must be in U.S. dollars, checks payable to the American Family Foundation.* To order, send a list of requested items with costs in parentheses, total the items, include your name, address, and phone number, enclose check or money order for the total amount, and mail to AFF Information Service, P.O. Box 2265, Bonita Springs, FL 33959.

Periodicals

Cultic Studies Journal. Semiannual scholarly journal, now in its ninth year. Averages 100 pages per issue. (See reprints section below for sample article topics.) Individuals: $15.00 ($22.00); Institutions: $25.00 ($29.00). The only scholarly journal dealing with cults and psychological manipulation.

The Cult Observer. Review of media investigations and reports on cultic groups and psychological manipulation (10 issues/yr.) $30.00 ($42.00). Subscribers also receive the AFF Annual Report and *Young People and Cults. The Cult Observer* has reviewed over 2000 press accounts since 1979. *Cult News Highlights*, a four-page annual summary of *The Cult Observer*, is free to journalists and others upon request.

Young People and Cults. Semiannual newsletter providing news and advice to help clergy, educators, and others conduct preventive education programs for youth. Free to *Cult Observer* subscribers.

Back issues of the *Cultic Studies Journal* and *The Cult Observer* are available (some issues available only in photocopy format). *Cultic Studies Journal:* $7.50 ($11.00) per issue. *The Cult Observer:* $3.00 ($4.00) per issue.

---

* Amounts in parentheses indicate the contribution asked for air-mail orders outside North America.

Books and Special Resources

Cults: Saying "No" Under Pressure. Videotape anchored and narrated by Charlton Heston (25 minutes). Co-produced by the National Association of Secondary School Principals, Instructivision, Inc., and the International Cult Education Program, a joint program of AFF and the Cult Awareness Network. Useful teaching tool focusing on psychological manipulation and how to resist it. VHS only; purchase only, no rentals. $78.00 ($83.00). Discounted price to AFF contributors: $62.00 ($67.00).

Satanism and Occult-Related Violence: What You Should Know. Michael D. Langone, Ph.D., & Linda Blood. (1990). 120-page book providing an overview of Satanism and advice for parents and helping professionals. $13.00 ($15.00).

Cults: Questions and Answers. Michael D. Langone, Ph.D. (1988). Succinct overview. 13 pages. $3.00 ($4.00).

Resource List. List of organizations, mental health professionals, clergy, attorneys, and law enforcement personnel with cult-related experience. Free upon request with purchase of any AFF publication or periodical.

Information Packets

Most packets contain 50–90 pages of journal, magazine, and newspaper articles about a particualr group or topic. Inclusion of a group does not necessarily mean that it is a cult or is destructive, only that we receive inquiries about it. Each packet: $12.00 ($14.00).

Group packets: •Ananda Marga •Bible Speaks •Church Universal and Triumphant •Children of God •Da Free John •Divine Light Mission •Eckankar •Est (Erhard Seminar Training; The Forum) •Hare Krishna •Healthy, Happy, Holy (3HO) •Lyndon LaRouche •Frederick Lenz/Rama •Lifespring •Maranatha •Roy Masters •Nichiren Soshu of America (NSA) •Rajneesh •Scientology •TM (Transcendental Meditation) •Unification Church (Moonies) •The Way International •Worldwide Church of God

Topic packets: •Bible-based groups •Business and the New Age movement •Child abuse in cults •Ethics of evangelism •Legal packet •Mental health packet •Neo-Nazi groups •New Age movement •Psychotherapy cults •Satanism •Sun Myung Moon and the Conservative movement

Reports

Destructive Cult Conversion: Theory, Research, and Treatment. John G. Clark, M.D. et al. (1981). 84 pages. $10.00 ($13.00).

Family Cult Questionnaire: Guidelines for Professionals. Michael D. Langone, Ph.D. (1983). 31 pages. $5.00 ($7.00).

Deprogramming: An Analysis of Parental Questionnaires. Michael D. Langone, Ph.D. (1984). 54 pages. $10.00 ($12.00).

New Religions and Public Policy: Research Implications for Social Scientists. Michael D. Langone, Ph.D., & John G. Clark, M.D. (1984). 42 pages. $5.00 ($7.00).

How Cults Affect Families. Henrietta and Curt Crampton. (1988). 4 pages. $2.00 ($3.00).

Cracking the Riddle of the Cults: Frontiers of Freedom in an Information Age. Flo Conway & Jim Siegelman (authors of *Snapping*). (1988). 12 pages. $2.00 ($3.00).

Business and the New Age Movement: Report of a Symposium. (1988). 4 pages. $2.00 ($3.00).

Satanism and Satanism-Related Crime: A Resource Guide. Linda O. Blood (1989). A very comprehensive bibliography and listing. 50+ pages. $5.00 ($7.00).

How Courts Work. Frederick Solomon, Esq. (1989). 4 pages. $1.00 ($2.00).

Cults: What Clergy Should Know. Rev. Richard L. Dowhower. (1989). 4 pages. $1.00 ($2.00).

Cultic Studies Bibliography. Partly annotated list of books and articles for researchers. Includes complete list of articles that have appeared in the *Cultic Studies Journal*. $3.00 ($4.00).

Reprints from the *Cultic Studies Journal*

Reprints are $3.00 ($4.00) each, unless otherwise indicated.

On Resisting Social Influence. Susan Andersen, Ph.D., & Philip Zimbardo, Ph.D. (1984). 23 pages.

The Vatican Report on Cults. (1986). 23 pages.

Cults Go To High School: A Theoretical and Empirical Analysis of the Initial Stage in the Recruitment Process. Philip Zimbardo, Ph.D., & Cynthia Hartley, M.A. (1985). 56 pages. $4.00 ($5.00).

Brainwashing and the Moonies. Geri-Ann Galanti, Ph.D. (1984). 10 pages.

Ritualistic Abuse of Children: Dynamics and Impact. Susan J. Kelley, Ph.D. (1988). 10 pages.

Cultism: A Conference for Scholars and Policymakers. Louis J. West, M.D., & Michael D. Langone, Ph.D. (1986). Report of a Wingspread conference conducted by AFF and UCLA's Neuropsychiatric Institute. 16 pages.

Litigation Advice from Experienced Attorneys. (1986).

Cults and the Law: A Report of the National Legal Seminar, III. (1988).

Litigating the Cult-Related Child Custody Case. Randy Frances Kandel, J.D., Ph.D. (1988).

Litigating Child Custody with Religious Cults. Ford Greene, Esq. (1989).

Prosecuting an Ex-Cult Member's Undue Influence Suit. L. Levy, J.D.

Psychotherapy Cults. M. T. Singer, Ph.D., M. Temerlin, Ph.D., & M. Langone, Ph.D.

Persuasive Techniques in Contemporary Cults: A Public Health Approach. L.J. West, M.D.

Legal Analysis of Intent as a Continuum Emphasizing Social Context of Volition. Herbert L. Rosedale, Esq.

State of Israel Report of the Interministerial Committee Set Up to Examine Cults ("New Groups") in Israel. $4.00 ($5.00).

The Use of Hypnotic Techniques in Religious Conversion. Jesse Miller, Ph.D.

The Effects of Religious Cults on Western Mainstream Religions. M. Rudin & Rabbi A. J. Rudin.

Family Responses to a Young Adult's Cult Membership and Return. L. Goldberg, M.S.W., and W. Goldberg, M.S.W.

Task Force Study of Ritual Crime. Virginia State Crime Commission, Michael Maddox, Esq.

Cults, Evangelicals, and the Ethics of Social Influence. Special issue (1985). $7.50 ($11.00).

Teaching Aids

Cults and Mind Control. Six-page educational handout for students and others. Excerpts from selected publications. Resource list. Single copy: $1.00 ($1.50); 30 copies: $8.00 ($10.00); 100 copies: $23.00 ($28.00).

Cultivating "Cult Evading": A Teacher's Guide. Sandy Andron, Ed.D. Flexible curriculum guide. (1983). 44 pages. $10.00 ($12.00).

How To Talk To People Who Are Trying To Save You. Rev. Dr. Ross Miller. 4 pages. Single copy: $1.00; 30 copies: $5.00 ($7.00); 100 copies: $15.00 ($22.00).

When You're Asked About Cults. Robert C. Fellows, M.T.S. 4 pages. Single copy: $1.00; 30 copies: $5.00 ($7.00); 100 copies: $15.00 ($22.00).

Easily Fooled: New Insights and Techniques for Resisting Manipulation. Robert C. Fellows, M.T.S. A magician explains the deceptions in everyday life. $6.00 ($8.00).

Pseudoscience Fact Sheets: Resources to Promote Critical Thinking. Produced by the Austin Society to Oppose Pseudoscience (with the assistance of AFF). Brief papers on such topics as astrology, extrasensory perception, spiritualism, astral travel, and other subjects. (1988). 43 pages. $5.00 ($7.00).

Additional Books by AFF Committee Members

(ordering instructions follow each listing)

The Anatomy of Illusion. Thomas W. Keiser, Ph.D., J.D., & Jacqueline L. Keiser, M.S.W. (1987). 160 pages. $29.95. Charles C. Thomas Publisher, 2600 S. First St., Springfield, IL 62794.

The History of Conversion and Contemporary Cults. Natalie Isser, Ph.D., & Lita Linzer Schwartz, Ph.D. (1988). 230 pages. $34.50. Peter Lang Publishing, Inc., 62 W. 45th St., New York, NY 10036.

Non-Profit and Charitable Solicitation in Canada: A Review of Techniques and Ethical Considerations. (1986). 170 pages. $18.00. Cult Project, 5655 Park Avenue, H2V 4H2 Montreal, Quebec, Canada.

Painted Black: From Drug Killings to Heavy Metal. Carl Raschke, Ph.D. (1990). 276 pages. $16.95. Harper SanFrancisco, 1160 Battery Street, San Francisco, CA 94111.

About the Publisher

The **American Family Foundation** (AFF) is a non-profit, tax-exempt research and educational organization founded in 1979 to assist cult victims and their families through the study of cultic groups and manipulative techniques of persuasion and control. AFF shares its findings with professionals, the general public, and those needing help with cultic involvements.

AFF consists of a small professional staff and approximately one hundred volunteer professionals, including psychiatrists, psychologists, educators, sociologists, social workers, physicians, attorneys, clergy, journalists, business executives, law enforcement officials, college and university administrators, scientists, and others who contribute their efforts in the areas of research, education, the law, and victim assistance.

For more information, write

American Family Foundation
P.O. Box 2265
Bonita Springs, FL 33959